ONE DAY
SOON
by
Deborah Brooks Langford
AF476565
© SonnetWolf Designs

# ONE DAY SOON

DEBORAH BROOKS LANGFORD

COVER DESIGN BY
SUSAN JOYNER-STUMPF

.

ISBN PAPERBACK: 978-1-304-63982-0

THIS BOOK WAS CREATED USING THE LULU PUBLISHING SERVICE

PUBLISHED BY DESTINY TO WRITE PUBLICATIONS
BARRY MOWLES – CARDIFF, WALES, UK

PRINTED BY LULU.COM

Author Deborah Brooks Langford

# DEDICATION PAGE

I am so excited my Fourth Poetry book "One Day Soon"
I want to dedicate this book to my Father War Veteran Bill Brooks that just passed away. He went on to be with the Lord on June 30, 2013
Without My father's love and his encouragement and support I would not have pursued my dreams.
He believed in me when I did not.
I want to thank my family my sons Jason and Aaron and their wonderful families and my friends that told me to hurry up and get it published. And my sweet Husband Van that is so devoted to me.
God Bless You all!
Most of all My Lord and Savior Jesus Christ for saving my life

# ABOUT THE AUTHOR

Author and Poet Deborah Brooks Langford
When I was in 5th grade my teacher introduced me to books. Jane Eyre wuthering heights... etc... I fell in love with books... They took me on adventures and I would daydream... And I started writing...
I have been writing poems all my life. When I was in school I would write instead of listen and dream of different poems and stories. My passion is poetry. I love to write and if I don't write I feel very depressed. Writing my poetry and stories helps me emotionally.
I was born in North Carolina, I am a military brat. We lived in Germany and Spain and Turkey. My father's side of the family comes from Cherokee North Carolina and my mother's families are English.
I dedicated everything I do in the memory of my wonderful sweet mother and to Jesus Christ My Lord and Savior.
I have written three poetry books.
"My Heart I give"
"Silenced Hearts" Createspace and on amazon,
"Break Of A New Dawn"
Plus my new Novel "Brooke".
The sequel to "BROOKE", IS "BROOKE AND NICK". It is almost finished…
And the third book in the series. "Brooke Forever" is Brooke in her younger days
I am working on children's books too. Nine in all…..
Plus I am working on cookbooks……
My new cook book will be out soon
Called:
"Debi's Magic Kitchen and Her Fabulous Friends."

I love working for our country. I am very passionate about that. I love working with the veterans. My father is a veteran from Pork chop in the Korean War and two tours in Vietnam and just recently my father Sgt. Bill Brooks just died at age of 83.

I married my sweet husband from high school, He is retired from the Navy.

Look for me Deborah Brooks Langford on Createspace and amazon.com and Lulu.com

# CONTENTS

For My Spanish family

# ONE DAY SOON

One day I will find you
One day you will be mine
Gently you will caress my life
Our shadows will whisper of love
Going deeper and slowly in the pain
Losing my best friend one more day
The picture being drawn brings us to shame
Just one more day,
Like searing color on immortal Day.
The masterpiece artist will draw our love,
Just one more day
One Day Soon
You will be there,
One more time, in my heart, My Love

Un día antes
un día lo voy a encontrar que un día
te
acaricie suavemente, mi vida
nuestra sombra será un susurro de amor
va más profundo y lentamente en el dolor
perder a mi mejor amigo un día más
la imagen que se extrae de la vergüenza nos trae
sólo un día más, como un color en inmortal
Día. la obra maestra artista dibujar nuestro amor, solo un día
más.

Un día antes de tiempo,
será,
una vez más, en mi corazón
mi amor.

Debbie

# SHE WAS BUT FIFTEEN

*She was but a child*
*But a sweet teen*
*She was kind of wild*
*Full of desire*
*Excited about love*
*In the ivory palaces of her mind*
*There rose up a white dove:*
*With a fury*
*Flawless in a never changing*
*World*
*She was just fifteen...*

# HELLO, YOU CAN CALL ME SAMANTHA

That's the day she ran away
This is the first day of the rest of my life and it might be my last.
Imagine me this day, maybe I wasn't the best kid in school, and I always felt alone. I didn't try very hard because I never had anything to work for, and I always dreamed. Dreamed about becoming anything other than I was.
The child abuse that I endured, the rape later on, Was it too much to bear? You bet it was!
That's when I ran away. The pain was just too much.
*Because a house is not a home*
*No One there*
*To hold me*
*Tight*
*A house*
*Is not a home*
*So please*
*Don't tell me*
*That happiness*
*Is gone*
*When a house is not a*
*Home....*

You see that house with the kids playing and daddy is smiling and mommy loving? That is not my home.
Where it's fun to live, the noise would be too deafening of laughter in my throat.
Where tears are all I knew, so from this day forward she flew

*To be no more;*
*Simple white roses*
*Tangled*
*In her golden hair*
*Her crown of thorns*
*Bloodstains*
*Her angelica*
*Face*
*So torn*
*Free so free*
*Angels*
*Fall sometimes*
*Angels*
*Even*
*Cry or die....*

Where was she to go? Running away to a nowhere ending, There were no roses, no violets, and no violins. Only pain and no surrender;
Her mother died at age 10 she thinks in 19 something, her memory wasn't that good anymore and then the abuse started. All she knew is that her mom had been dying for years and her father was a very angry man. Samantha was the one her father took the anger out on.

Actually her mom died when she was born, and then at three a little more, then at seven lots more and then at ten she was in the ground.
As far she recalled her mom has been slipping away for years. Slipping, slipping and slipping. The casket just made it official.
She was always just out of reach. So you see she had a ten year lifetime of the inevitable.
When she left for the last time sleeping that last sleep of forever and enduring of five years of her father's raping her and beating her.
This day she just walked out!
Samantha did not care where she went.
A short lifetime of regrets, goodbyes, longings and yearnings and wanting love that was never meant to be:
How long does Samantha just keep on dying with her? How long?
As her head lay down next to her mom's that fateful day.
That's the day she ran away;

# A THOUSAND ROSES FOR YOU

My eyes read the beautiful words
My heart felt each and every touch
Making all the sweet songs of birds
With each breath I breathe I feel
Your words make me long for your beauty
The symbols of longing that appeal
For each single smile…..

I want to give you a thousand Roses
But believe me you deserve more
Taking photos of the light
With each word you write
My heart cries and aches
Wanting more it says making no mistakes….

The kiss of life is in your words
So lovely and on my cheek I feel
The grass stained dress silks my mind
And many more as flames of night
As the years go by dreams fall into place….

I slip my scarf to cover my heart
The butter that churns my will
I don't understand the chill
Reading such beauty comes to life
A thousand roses just for you….
The beauty took over my life
From the words of precious love
Each page takes new beauty
That meets each bright day
More and More I read I see
Thousand Roses Just For You…..
*Hugs and kisses and much love*
*Debbie*

# HOLDING FIRM

Holding to your love, and never letting go wishing and wanting strongly of kisses forever more. No more tears, never letting go.

Crimson sea
*Mystery*

*Burning heart*

*Blocked*

*Lives change*

*So much blame*

*Holding firm'*

*From above*

*Being in love*

*True hearts*

*Highest heights*

*Deep sea shadows*

*Singing Zion*

*Heavens sanctum*

*Sacred gold*

*Lovers running*

*Under covers*

*So much fun*

*Love letters*

*To my soul*

*Golden era*

*Faces taunted*

*Tears*

*Aglow*

*Enlightened*

*To my dance*

*Holding your heart*

*One more triumph*

*My life souring*

*To your sound*

*Holding firm*

*One more time……*

# FORWARD IN TIME

Nothing in our world is so unyielding then the inexorable march of time
What would happen when man finds a way to manipulate that awesome force?
The world
As we see it, shut
Up against our will, Deprived
Of all contact, the strictness Abandoned
For the world
The unbearable
Has appeared despite
All the praying Passion of
One so young, Christ gives different
Challenges To different souls, to be blessed
Not all
Of it is pretense
In those love starving
Nights there have been
Things there, things she saw
Half formed shapes growing out
Of shadows sudden auras Flashes of light
At the edge
Of her vision'
As the fool begins
The wits are gone, all
That honored, despised her
They have seen the shame, a kind
Of stillness, hangs over the land
The atmosphere remains
Unchanged she is

Waiting
Her soul remains intact
Despite the warnings of
Distant lands, she had wept into
The night, her tears were on her cheeks
Abbess must be brought to the plan, watching
Her loose her grip, with sharp eyes under no illusion
Coming to confess her disobedience visiting
The novice at night, breaking the great
Silence, in the City of Ark Angels
Forward in time becomes her
Dark red love falls all
Around, cross the
Courtyard
She held a candle
For him in the shadowed
That burns into the night
Breathing him
Breathing her,
Is brighter
Forward in
Time!
Some men loose themselves in War
Others find themselves…

# THE SURVIVAL OF THE HEART

The heart is so delicate and so tender, and all though love might fly away, somehow the heart will survive.

*To transcend time and space*
*To bring forth all that's holy*
*The heart will survive*
*Although love has flown*
*Deafening to her life*
*With grace and eloquence*
*Is the survival of the heart....*
*Both real and imagined*
*Attempt to sustain their love*
*In a brutal world of beauty*
*The sound of the heart*
*A magnificent tale of woe*
*Alone can bridge vast charms of life*
*When they fall in love*
*The survival of the heart*
*Forever and ever it will be*
*With the heart for now*
*And the heart will survive*
*But as the darkness*
*Which every day looms*
*With deafening lightness*
*Begging the heart to come back*
*With loyalty, strength and betrayal*
*But faith in the future*
*Is the survival of the Heart!*

*This is dedicated to my friend Poet and Author Susan Joyner Stumpf, she had such a sad life when she was young, and my heart breaks for her. Susan I love you*

# A TINY FACE

The Face in the painting is a face of a little girl that she sees constantly. Day and Night, she sees the little face in the mirror, and in the painting, wondering who the little one is. Is she the little one she lost long ago or is she the face of herself?

She was a face in a painting a Face
Hidden Within
Each painting, the
Heart still beating, the
Mystery surrounding Broken to begin
Relationships Breathtaking mysteries
With her little face, always there in the midst
Of stolen lives Outbursts with angry eyes with emotion
Locked with blood pounding in her face as she
Dreamed of the little face, in the painting
The sad little face with tear drops falling
Causing the emotion that took her
Breathe away. The little hand
Reaching for the mother
She never had
The love
Laugher
Little Child in the painting sad and hungry she was
Never there
Hurt that lined

Her face, in the painting
Starving for food, for love
Tears pooled her little eyes
So much pain to overcome till
The next time she couldn't move
Because of hunger hurting her tummy
The ground was softened by rain by the tree
As she laid her head one last time with
One last tear falling, her limbs
Stiffened with coldness
Never to be found
And so the face
Be told as she
Laid in the
Painting
Of
Life…..

# TO FEEL YOU BESIDE ME AGAIN

Meeting the one, You thought would be forever in your life, when one day after all the love and promises, then that person is gone, and having to go on emotionally and physically

*It was the touch of August*
*That you swept into my life*
*Remembering*
*The warmth*
*The touch*
*The holding on*
*Feeling your breath*
*Keeps me dreaming of love*
*Contentment for a peaceful life*
*No turning back I know my lover*
*Remembering the beauty of our time*
*With a melting heart I do hear*
*Feeling a loneliness that comes*
*With a soft moan, of the passion*
*My memory of you shall never dim*
*I don't see you, my heart screams*
*I remember the kisses the love*
*The promises of yes's*
*Lonely nights I sit and stare*
*With darkness staring back at me*
*Longing for your touch*
*Wanting the kiss of your lips*
*With the comfort to hold*
*I woke up today*

*Realized the promises*
*Were of the past, so no more*
*Promises do I need with the loneliness*
*No more touching*
*No more laughter*
*No more your breath*
*To carry me on*
*My path will not carry me to you*
*My path will end here*
*With you not beside me*
*No more promises*
*No more breath*
*I resolve*
*This is the end*
*No more love*
*And no more feeling you beside me*
*This is the end.....*

# AFTER THE SUMMER RAIN

A summer romance of long ago, meeting again years later and all the memories come rushing back, in the summer rain.

*After the summer rain*
*After the rain you were there*
*Against the rainbow of magic*
*Crawl with me through the dawn*
*Hold me and let's watch the wind*
*I want you to remember*
*What might, could have been.*
*What might be forever more?*
*Now the memory blurs*
*In quite the same way*
*As the touch fades so ever slightly*
*Oh it's the rainbow bridge*
*A patch of august light…*
*The summer is over*
*But sweet songs come forth.*
*Maybe there are no more doors*
*Hopefully this is it.*
*Let no one kill our rainbows.*
*Although the world rarely sees,*
*I'm not sure that even the slow death of time*
*Can be the master of misrepresented.*
*I am not sure that I could say with certainty*
*The love that flew away*
*And the eagles of tomorrow;*
*Perhaps there is a slight ache in the air.*
*The pain of long lost gain;*

*The touch that left me breathless*
*The look of so longed days*
*Through the grove of cottonwoods;*
*The ache the pain of not having*
*The look of long ago;*
*Letting the sun get into our brains*
*To fill us with sun love*
*That is ripening in your touch.*
*To slowly touch your face*
*To hold the other so tight*
*It has been some time ago*
*That at the start of one certain summer;*
*Besides we are not so old*
*To be mystified with flowers*
*AFTER the summer rain…*

# CHASING THE LONELY

The Lonely in this world are so alone. The beggars, the desperate that need help, as they disappear into the night. As they end up dead and alone.

*Desperate for help*
*Determined to regain*
*True desire of the heart*
*Despite the circumstances*
*Undeniable attraction with the beauty*
*Surprised to discover the struggling*
*In a land of loyalties divided*
*In a country ravaged by*
*War, of the making*
*Of any hope*
*Where a*
*Blush*
*Love*
*Can survive*
*Begging on the street*
*Meaning to be a meager*
*Pickings that had been waiting*
*For life to take him by the hand*
*With scanned lines quickly dropped and*
*Disappeared, as he fell dead*
*Only the Lonely*
*Oh the Lonely*
*Only the lonely knows*
*The night, the tears are*
*For them, with beating hearts*
*Then disappeared into the night*

*'Are you going to die?' Is the raging question*
*'One day sure', is the valuable answer*
*As they made their way to the*
*Gravesite of the falling*
*Dead*
*Everyone dies they said*
*Even the Lonely, chasing their*
*Dreams, to the extreme of time*
*Knowing the battle would take place*
*In the forever land this night of the evil lies*
*Sunshine had warmed their faces*
*Clouds had drifted north*
*Horses rested for a while*
*As the children played*
*The wailing had started*
*Straining to hear*
*What only the*
*Lonely, could*
*Know*
*Tears*
*As they were chasing the dearly departed*
*That was the lonely....*

*'This poem is dedicated to my sweet friend that lives in Colorado, Poet and Author Susan Joyner Stumpf.... She loves wolfs.'*

# THE BLOODY RED SKY MOON

Under the Bloody red sky, and a lost lass finds a white wolf
and a love develops under the bloody moon.
Bloody moon
To a delight
So far away
As the land deteriorates
WITH THE RED MOON
People seek the knowledge
With one chance of survival
Is the return of love abound
But nowhere to be found
Where magic and determination
Will come to pass
The search will lead them
To a simple shy lass
Hiding from the world
Behind her books
And daily life
And her smiles come….
In remembrance of
The awesome lonely wolf
Howling at the moon
That sleeps like a baby
Like a cartoon character
Stalking the prey

With the slick white hair
Was the beautiful white wolf
As the white wolf looks for the lass
Rolling over and over again
Licking her face
As she lets her mind relaxed
To slide her consciousness to her reality
To be destined to be a true companion
A protector in his own right
The wolf following the lass
Like a puppy
Standing at the lake
Enjoying the pure splendor of the midnight site
With the red sky foaming with the moon
As they stood there in the night…………..

*'This is dedicated to my sweet Mom that went on to be with the Lord on July 2011'*

# HER NAME WAS BARBARA ROSE

This is dedicated to My Mom in Heaven for Mother's Day
*'Happy Mother's Day in Heaven, from your daughter Deborah Jo.'*
*My Mother in Heaven on Mother's Day*
*A Mom in Heaven*
*The many tears she dried*
*Her arms so strong*
*As she would hold me tight*
*The hands so sweet*
*As she sang a lullaby*
*Her children she loved*
*Far and wide*
*Her neighbors she treated*
*With pride*
*She taught all about Jesus*
*As she bent her knees*
*Now she is in heaven*
*Singing Glory Halleluiah*
*She taught me to speak my thoughts*
*To paint the world*
*With my canvas*
*The moon has risen*
*As she tucked me into bed*
*One last time as she went bye bye*
*Welcome Barbara Rose*

*I Miss you So Much*
*If you were still alive*
*I would give you a rose like your name that you deserve*
*All that you did for me*
*All that you did for Love*
*My Mom, Barbara Rose*
*'You were the best Mom ever, not only to me and our brothers and sisters you made strangers feel like they were one of us.'*
*You name was a flower and so were you.*
*Your scent was an aroma that drew all far and wide*
*Mom I love you then and I love you now*
*You taught me to hold on to the moments*
*Hold on to*
*Memories*
*Even if they are sad*
*Make sure I hold on to*
*Love.....*
*I remember you brushing my hair*
*Telling me I could have the world*
*But I needed THE SON first*
*So Mom I reach to find your hand*
*And Praise Our Lord for the blessing*
*Of having you for a MOM!*
*Then you were gone*
*The Day You died*
*So Hot the Day*
*The Day You went away...*
*Then you were none*
*The day was hot*
*You were in the ground*
*The tears were shed*
*As I saw you standing there*

*Waving good bye*
*"Please don't cry"*
*You whispered to me*
*I am happy, no more pain*
*You were a good daughter*
*And mom you are the best*
*But what am I going to do?*
*With my loss....*
*You always said*
*"If God is for us, who can be against us?"*
*God thank you, but I am weak*
*I need my mom*
*On this eventful day*
*Mother's day is here*
*And it will come and go*
*But the pain is real*
*But the joy of having a mom*
*Like you!*
*Is a Blessing to me!*
*For ever more!*

# HE WAS HER FAIRYTALE

*'She remembered him as a Fairytale, ever since the day he went away. She could not move on so the years tolled past her as her dreams began to fade, dreaming of her fairytale.'*

*He was her dream*
*He was her fairytale*
*Whenever he was around*
*She wondered if he felt it*
*The magic in the air*
*It started with a smile*
*That went on for a mile*
*He was her Fairytale*
*Once upon a time was a long time ago*
*He was her fairytale...*
*But those days are long gone*
*And now is forever more*
*She sees him in her dreams*
*Sitting in the church reading the word*
*As her heals dragged the floor*
*And the smell of coffee cooking*
*As The chair was pulled up*
*By his side*
*Oh love*
*The surprise of adoration*
*Shown on his face*
*In a blink of an eye*
*Oh how times have changed*
*Sparks use to fly*
*Before he went away*
*Was he dreaming about her?*

*Like she was dreaming of him?*
*She chased away the tear*
*In a blink of an eye*
*The fairytale was grand*
*With his loving hand*
*Stroking her heart*
*So many different ways*
*Ah the memories of the fairytale*
*Yesterday's smile*
*Was so grand*
*As the soft kiss met*
*It was a wonderful time*
*It was a fairytale*
*As the years went by*
*She waited for her fairytale*
*To return*
*As the tears dragged on*
*Never to resume*
*The Fairytale*
*She let herself believe Miracles could happen*
*As the dream dreamed on*
*And the love bleeds deeper*
*The tears dried up*
*And the fairytale wades past her*
*Standing in the church seeing his head*
*Bowed to the Son*
*With her arms hanging*
*Wanting to resume*
*Tears sliding slowly*
*Never to overcome*
*As time slowly came*

*To her fairytale*
*The day still haunts her*
*Like it was yesterday*
*Those fall and winter days*
*Maybe it wasn't worth the pain*
*As the smile fades fast and*
*The tears resume*
*With the pain striking hard*
*Just wanting her FAIRYTALE….*

# MY EMPTINESS

*'This is about a broken heart crying out to the Lord for forgiveness.'*

*Dear Father*
*A mustard seed you said...*
*Used to symbolize the greatest of a faith*
*One lost coin you spoke*
*Used to depict God's love*
*A little shepherd boy that became a king*
*Cried to his Lord...*
*But me Lord, I am praying*
*Because*
*I have an aching heart*
*I know I have ignored you lately*
*Can you forgive me?*
*I know I haven't been a good person*
*For you to look at*
*Can YOU forgive this sinner?*
*But my tears are real*
*My heart is broken*
*How do I say I am sorry?*
*Your love never grows cold*
*Fill my emptiness with You Lord*
*The hearts that is broken*
*Is not funny!*
*The hurt that grows*
*I think back to the time I ask you My Lord*
*Into my heart*

*Those were happy times*
*I ask you again*
*To help my heart*
*You walked the earth with constant demands*
*But YOU are God....*
*I want what you have*
*Into your hands I commit*
*I need your peace Lord*
*I need, I need, and I need*
*Please Lord, Be all I need!*
*Please take me to a deserted spot*
*To rest a while*
*Help me lift my eyes to YOU!*
*Don't forget me Lord*
*I need you NOW!*
*You are my everything.....*
*I have thrown love away*
*I don't want to throw YOU away*
*I want the happiness*
*I want the love*
*I want YOU!*
*'The Lord is good to those that wait on HIM, to the soul who seeks HIM!'*
*Lamentations 3:25*

# I SHOULD HAVE TOLD YOU MY HEART

*'This poem is about finding the perfect Love only to lose him. The pain and torment she goes through is devastating.'*

*In the misty morning*
*My heart is breaking*
*Where did it go?*
*The brokenness*
*Wishing I told you*
*More*
*Why did I wait?*
*To tell you my*
*Love*
*Just know I will always love you*
*Falling in love was*
*So new*
*Falling on my face makes*
*Me blue*
*You were gone*
*You found someone*
*Too*
*I fall asleep*
*I see your face....*
*Always with your hat in your hand*
*I see*
*I fell in love*
*With you*

*All I can say is*
*I love you*
*I will be a friend*
*As long as you want me to*
*Be.....*
*When you are blue*
*I will cheer you*
*I will sing to you*
*If you just ask me*
*Too*
*Our love was special*
*But I threw it away*
*I was buried alive in your*
*Love*
*I felt so secure*
*Yesterday it ended*
*Today is gone*
*So much as happened*
*Trying to remember all*
*Your sweet words*
*The stars were blinking*
*As you walked by*
*The day stood still*
*I'm biting my lip*
*I try not to cry*
*I wanted to go to the beach*
*It did not happen*
*Everything seemed to come in our way*
*Maybe or maybe*
*It's God's will?*

*So my darling, I guess this is*
*Goodbye*
*As I fall madly in love still!*
*Debbie*

# ONE DAY YOU LOVE ME, THE NEXT DAY YOU DON'T

*Yesterday you said you love me*
*Today you don't*
*The hurt that's in my heart*
*You painted out our mountains*
*And told me about the trees*
*You narrowed my world*
*For me you said*
*Though we know*
*Our gaze was on each other*
*Today it's lost forever*
*Our tomorrows are gone now*
*On this seventh day*
*There are no smiles*
*There is a place I frequent for you*
*In search for the love*

*In hope you will find me*
*There are no smiles*
*There is a place I frequent for you*
*In search for the love*
*In hope you will find me*
*And our hearts will merge*
*I am a prisoner to your world my love*
*What am I to do now?*
*Now hollow and empty*
*Are your feelings towards me!*
*Memories elapse*

*Words no longer savored*
*On the tongue*
*I am isolated from my present thoughts*
*Thinking of the love we had*
*So why are my eyes still crying?*
*When I feel like I need to die.*

*Debi*

# EVERYTHING WAS A BLUR THAT DAY

The Day you went away
*Melting like snow in the summer*
*Leaving me to wonder and not slumber*
*Was this moment a blur my friend?*
*Or was I a cancer like victim*
*Carrying an illness to date*
*That would plague me so late*
*With a curse just like this*
*I was to young too die I plead*
*Would I make it now?*
*Everything was a*
*Blur*
*I chose*
*To live another*
*So instead of making this*
*Life sentence today I say*
*I know my life wasn't destined*
*To end this way my friend*
*Understanding I had a chance*
*Gives me time to prepare*
*My way this day*
*I had cancer*
*I have*
*Life*
*I am*

*Wiser, smarter*
*Healthier and determined*
*To make this a better way*
*The Army of life Source*
*In this Army of Life*
*Holds the secret of strife*
*I am a survivor of likes*
*I am not going anywhere*
*Among the star filled nights*
*In the middle of the moonlight*
*Out comes the silhouette*
*As sly as a snake*
*Am I the person?*
*Who is always?*
*Hurting*
*I*
*Never planned*
*It this way come what may*
*It is a possibility*
*That I don't feel this insecurity*
*As everything was a blur that day...*

# THE DEATH OF ME I SEE

An introduction and poem about a woman's continuing dreams and visions about a continuing out of body experience.
Remembering my dreams of long ago
This is about remembering my dreams of long ago, dreaming of dying or falling and seeing my body on the ground. Embracing my dreams and or trying to understand what it is about. Plus just imagine what it would be like to see the Angels coming to hold my hand to help me make the transition a little bit easier. Then to see my Lord's face, the excitement and the questions I might have.
Just to enlighten my world's and my spirits just a little bit more with the possibilities of my dreams coming true and then not to be frighten what may lay ahead for me. My journey to heaven and the most pleasure that will come my way, and for the Lord to speak to my heart and for me to find the honor and love that I feel when I think about my Lord and seeing His face. As I bare my soul to my Lord I pray for His acceptance for this lowly servant that I am.
*So Lord here I am, there YOU are.*
*HOW HIGH I AM*
*Who is that I see?*
*Who is that over me?*
*My life is out on the ground*
*As my spirit lends restfully*
*I am in the near presence*
*Of the Lord I say?*
*As I float to and fro*
*Upon the beauty of the burning heart*
*AND*

*As the suns sets in the east*
*And place the moon on the horizon*
*I see myself*
*I think it's me*
*Or is it somebody else?*
*The clouds are coming on*
*Chariots,*
*To be weighed on scales of life*
*And the tongues of angels*
*Singing*
*To the heart of whispers*
*And floating over to and fro*
*Is the likes of me*
*Lord I say where is I?*
*Don't let this earth capture me*
*When love knocks*
*On my door*
*And I will dwell*
*AS I*
*To the pursuit of your justice*
*Dear Lord I ask I say*
*Who is that on the ground?*
*The angels have sown the sky*
*With lips that speak so gently*
*To let me know your there*
*As I look upon my form*
*I reach for your grace this day*
*So Lord, is that me on the ground?*
*As I look upon?*
*Floating with the Angels as I watch above;*
*Just how HIGH AM I?*

# BEAUTIFUL DARK WOMAN

*The beauty of the night, looking for solace here and there,*
*Wanting only love, wanting only new;*
*Needing the security of his handsome arms,*
*But fleeing for her life;*
*She being so beautiful and looking like an angel.*
*Beautiful Dark Woman*
*She sat thinking*
*What it was to be a lover*
*She prayed for soft scents*
*But she had a hollow heart*
*And an empty stomach*
*Her chest ache*
*Her arms so lonely*
*What is like living in a dramatic whirl!*
*Has she loved the unloved at fifteen?*
*Her spirit was too old*
*So she settled*
*Sleeping in his empty arms*
*Wanting to run for her life;*
*What she never understood*
*Is what her parents would deny*
*Her spell was a curse*
*In a new world where*
*Her own ship has sailed.*
*In rooms of old memories*
*Wanting the kiss*
*But not now*
*The kiss of death*
*Not life.*

*Past hurts had rotted the foundation*
*Not meant to last*
*A night mare of a*
*Free dream-smell of the air;*
*Fragile bonding, vulnerable*
*To the slightest pleasure*
*Where did the sun go?*
*Then it was a winter miracle*
*As the years rolled by*
*Being with the white light cast*
*Through the varicolored, painted glass,*
*Emerging from a self-same essence;*
*Then came the blow*
*She's been slipping astray*
*Death came between them*
*And took him away;*
*How will she live?*
*Why couldn't he stay?*
*So stead and unwavering*
*Is her love*
*So what is it like to be a lover?*
*So tender and new!*
*So beautiful dark woman*
*Your beauty knows no bounds.*
*Your heart beats for him*
*With each unique and holy dance*
*Unites In scared whole*
*As it is enhanced*
*And merge together here once more.*
*Beautiful pure dark woman,*

*Your loneness means so much*
*Disturbing calm*
*Chilling and moaning*
*In a deep shadow*
*That caught her suddenly*
*Now as the light glows*
*From afar this night*
*In its blue dim of the only haven*
*Ivy green as mighty*
*That carves out a twisted path road*
*To her heart;*
*Like a hallowed spot*
*The light rips open crazy clouds*
*She stares at the moon*
*At the Iron Gate;*
*Powerful and lean was he*
*Her hand stretched to his*
*As he disappeared into the dewy night;*
*To be adored are you*
*Of life's exhaling breathe;*
*With luminous fibers within*
*That is so you*
*Beautiful precious Dark Woman.*

# THE SWEET MEADOWS OF MY LIFE

A poem of memory about love and life
She Was Always Wondering About Love
She was always wondering about Love, as she strolled through the meadow that day. Why was it always so cruel? She did not know or understand.
She was getting close to down town and it was getting dark and the trains were running she realized. A street car, wonderfully modeled, shot off the tracks racing through intersections; it was wheeling out into the forest and back into town. Was love on the streetcar? Was he there?
She was finally on Oak Street and it was real dark by now, you could hear the whispering fall of individual pine needles as they dropped in the woods.
Then she saw him as she neared her home, she felt herself suck in her breath. She thought is this a dream or a nightmare? He started towards her; she wondered why he is here? All she wanted to do was run and hide. She didn't want him to hurt her any more. She did not want to hear his lies. Or feel the back of his hand.

She stopped in her tracks as he approached her. She dropped her packages and turned to run, but at last he could run faster. He let her go. He did not pursue her. She looked back thinking he is not there, when out of nowhere there he was with his hands around her throat. Hurting her and laughing at her. How could she have ever thought she loved this man? How could he want to hurt her like this? Her man was gone again after leaving her to die.

*Love you are unforgiving*
*And unkind you are*
*Love you are cruel*
*And frugal*
*Withholding my blessings*
*Love you promised me the world*
*You were going to be gentle*
*And unconditional*
*Instead you took*
*The sweet meadows of my life*
*And made it rain.*
*Shroud in mists*
*Across the straits where lovers cry*
*Flanks smooth as silk*
*As love smiled and called my name*
*My hair loosely pulled back*
*I brought up one graceful arm*
*As my fingers danced over your alluring skin*
*And our twin hearts*
*Poured out the songs*
*Of the swaying strings*
*And smiled and called his name.*
*Summer has come and gone.*
*I writhe to free myself from*
*His grasp*
*I lift my face to the sun*
*With the warm rays of life giving skin*
*I cry*
*And search my soul for you*
*Holding fast and*
*Creeps in like thick oozing clay*

*A drug of memories for you*
*I say*
*Are the sweet meadows of my life.....*

# DADDY WHY DO YOU HURT ME SO?

This is dedicated to all those that suffer with children in the house and with an alcoholic in the family.

*My mommy cries daddy*
*Can't you see what you do to her and me?*
*You're drinking and yelling and cursing so*
*Makes me run and hide my eyes*
*My ears are sore and so is my heart*
*From what you do night after night;*
*You spend all your money that we need for food*
*On beer and fun that you say you need*
*I want to run so far away*
*But where would I go I ask myself*
*I pray to JESUS to help us so*
*I reach for HIS hand to not let me go*
*I wish my daddy would reach for us*
*And hold me and tell me he loves me now*
*Instead he wants his beer and fun and swearing.*
*If he could only take me to church I ask*
*And teach me about the one called JESUS.*
*But instead he would rather have his beer and friends,*
*I am tired of him yelling and falling down drunk*
*I want a daddy that wants me to.*
*So daddy I cry and cry today*
*But you never hear my sad word that I SAY*
*You just don't know how you hurt me so.*

*Other daddy's take their kids to the park*
*And other daddy's teach them how to play*
*Other daddy's keep their kids safe from harm*
*But my daddy doesn't care if I live or die.*
*Dear daddy why do you hurt me so.....*

# PURPLE MOONS

*Purple moon of you*
*With purple skies of new*
*With shapes that blaze a trail of love*
*To show the things that is yet to come.*
*The love it shows deep within.*
*The mountain pains to feel the way*
*Through frilly lisps of purple light*
*To bleed the blood of the night;*
*The purple sings the songs of old*
*Righteous that is known to know*
*Obvious freedom of living there*
*Among the purple icons so far and so near*
*Come autumn late and watch the night*
*The sun the moon and planets full.*
*To drink the glass of marble light*
*Walking alone at dawn*
*Seeing the purple that is a fright*
*Reaching for the slanted light*
*The purple Moon and purple night....*

# LIFE OF GOLD

*Oh the Art of letting go*
*You want me to do as I am told*
*Numbness and shaken*
*I cannot breathe*
*Listening to the fears*
*I feed*
*Touching your face*
*In a life to behold*
*Licking your wounds*
*Seeing you smile*
*Standing Tall*
*In this Life of gold*

# NO MORE FEARS

*Back in time I go*
*To a time*
*Of yesterdays*
*To a time of tomorrows*
*A chocolate soda with three scoops*
*Only a dime*
*20 years gone by*
*And then 40*
*Lots of memories*
*Do I recognize it?*
*Do I remember?*
*The life of some pain*
*Some happiness*
*Some remembrance*
*I think a lot of thoughts*
*I walk a lot of pavements*
*In my mind*
*Back in time I spent*
*Do I want to go?*
*Do I want to stay?*
*Put in a claim of my life*
*I had to go back.*
*I had to see for myself*
*Are they delusions?*
*Are they real?*
*What to do*
*The summer cottage*
*The spring rain*

*The love of my parents*
*The hurt of relatives*
*Riding the carousel*
*Running from my past*
*Trying to find a new one*
*Reaching for the unknown*
*It was a wonderful time of life*
*I let it go without enjoying it*
*No more merry go rounds*
*No more fears*
*No more concerts of my past*

# WEEPING RAIN

*The night is young*
*Pressure is on*
*Disillusions are ruined*
*Distant roar of forgiveness....*
*Never finds the perfection*
*Afloat in emptiness correction*
*Loves that is broken that*
*Needs His touch to heal....*
*The fading shadow it seems*
*Tears are in cemented dreams*
*Songs of despair of adulation*
*Takes a massacre of celebration....*
*Metal to flesh rushes the door*
*The feather of light wants more*
*Grace is known to reach the souls*
*Before my waking moments lose control...*
*Dreams are yet to come*
*The rain is weeping for our kind that become*
*Hiding hearts to their fate to say goodbye*
*Too weary for the passion to cry*
*God's tears cry too*
*Holding us in the palm of His hand*
*Sorry oh sorry as I hide on the stairs*
*Weeping rain for you and I....*

# GOODBYE

*Could tomorrow be worth it?*
*Just being alive makes it okay?*
*Seeing you in that casket brought such pain. .*
*Brings feelings with tears in my eyes*
*I wonder why I have to say good bye*
*The tears of frustration rolls down my face.*
*Why do we have to break down?*
*With life hanging on that one more thing might be said.*
*To tell you good bye!*

# FROM THIS MOMENT

Once love is true without the chains of death, can only be the true love of life…

*Taste from this time*
*Woman*
*From this moment on*
*Waste a single day*
*That her heart has won*
*Locking herself away*
*Underneath his protection*
*Holding one more day*
*Till the day came of lock and key*
*Much to her surprise*
*She had a hard time to see*
*The day came*
*Like a love so near*
*Only to hear the love song*
*So melodic and complete to bear*
*Holding hearts*
*Realizing no one can compare*
*Suffering…..*
*To no avail*
*Truth is all a lie*
*It's hard to believe*
*He would hurt her so*
*Weaving his words*
*Of love*
*Woe*
*Is he this day!*

*Scared of losing it all*
*Wants to turn her life around*
*Wants that special guy*
*To be on solid ground*
*Kissing beauty stars*
*Kissing beauty clears*
*Losing control*
*Lying on sensual bed*
*Loving so very deep*
*Their hearts once held*
*Once upon a time*
*He enlighten her world*
*With a book of beauty*
*In glory paradise*
*Illuminating the start of love*
*In the living sun*
*Their garden of love*
*Much to her surprise*
*Turned into a jail of many types*
*Of the holy shrines*
*Overstating the situation*
*He found out one day*
*The love he once had*
*Had fled at her expense*
*As she ran for her life*
*To see her dying day*
*Her heart spoke*
*Of love*
*Honor.....*
*And much respect*

*A knight of shining love*
*Came to her rescue*
*Picking up her dainty form*
*To place on his heart*
*Her eyes slowly open*
*To see*
*The beauty of true love*
*Before her lovely eyes*
*With a sip of a word*
*From this very moment*
*They will always love!*

# I HEARD A MAN

*I heard a man say the other day..*
*You don't about lonely*
*Until you have lived all your nights alone.*
*And the sadness that grabs your soul*
*Is the only*
*He sat there as I walked away....*
*The fear in my heart that I knew*
*The loss of my tears was not*
*Like the fear in that man's eyes.*
*The loss in my heart*
*As I listened to the wanting*
*The sound in my chest*
*Leading me astray*
*From fate into those arms*
*With a heart leading to passion*
*And the loneliness of my mind*
*With tears running down my soul*
*With*
*Only the Lonely*
*Memories fade and love still remains*
*Wounds will heal and pain will leave*
*The world consumes the deceiver souls*
*Anger misguided with wrought judgments*
*Eternity is cast into frigid dead coals*
*Eyes are weary*
*Body is weak*
*And my mind is dreary*
*But there is still lonely'*

*And still I go on*
*In this valley deep*
*But still I must sleep*
*But I will see what I will see*
*And I so hope that rests wait for me*
*We have so little to say in life*
*Saying words of hate and worthlessness*
*Expressing our souls*
*To windows that are open*
*To a constant view*
*Catching light and casting spells*
*Holding on to what one never tells*
*Sending words with simple glances*
*But there is still the lonely*
*The words of this man*
*Made my breath catch in my throat*
*With birds fluttering in my chest*
*I see myself reflected in his eyes*
*The love gone one last day*
*Living in this world together*
*We must stand and unite*
*A twin flame, of long ago*
*With love inside has no question*
*Our hearts will offer no suggestion*
*Still he said*
*There is only the Lonely.*

# SHE REMEMBERS HIS WORDS

*Do not be afraid*
*She heard him say*
*"I am here to hold you dear"*
*Her stillness became acquiescence to her still*
*It's nice to have you home for Christmas they may say*
*But her heart knows the better*
*The disgrace was still the footnote.*
*The night wind made a faint whisper*
*Telling her over and over*
*The time has come and gone*
*Forget the pain of evermore.*
*Dancing took her to a time*
*Her feet would fly and fly*
*Sweeping steps of every beat*
*To see those days that would go by;*
*Just to remember his words so dear*
*To clear her mind of pain*
*The slightest motion of his hand*
*To kiss the smiles she must be;*
*The sound reverberated through the crisp autumn air*
*Klung, klung, klung of the wood*
*Reminding her he was there.*
*She remembers his words although,*
*As the faint breeze lifted her veil*
*But the face she saw was the one captured of long ago;*
*With black skirts and pine needles that she wrote*
*The songs were sung to her heart*
*Etched forever more this day*

*With colored hair ribbons all so new*
*Ponytails askew;*
*He took her hand to strange places that were so few*
*On Saturday nights to kiss the kiss*
*She remembers the words he spoke*
*The bell tolled once and then twice she heard*
*Sound exploded and glass flew.*
*As her life fell around her like needles ever so slightly,*
*The pain of it all so gone*
*Just to remember the words he spoke;*
*The farther and farther he tolled*
*The longer and longer she was gone*
*So now the years have passed*
*The pain is as she remembers*
*And the WORDS HE SPOKE*
*Was so light*
*That it still tore her heart.*
*AS SHE REMEMBER HIS WORDS THIS NIGHT.*

# To My Spanish Friends and Family

Roto Estrellas Las Estrellas
me invitan
a sus brazos a este herido noche
yo podría decir que la luna se está muriendo de hambre me
para el
parpadeo y la caída
ha caído en amor con usted en
el descanso de la repentina
esta desesperación cae lentamente
como un tonto soy por su amor….

nuestras almas pueden evolucionar con
la rapidez de la luz
y las tinieblas se siga
amor es la manera
con
que el perdón es torturado y libre...

# BROKEN STARS

Stars beckon me
To your arms this wounded night
I could say the moon is starving me
For the blink and fall
Fallen into love with you
In the break of the suddenness
This despair drops slowly
As a fool I am for your love….

Our souls can evolve
With the suddenness of light
Then darkness will follow
Love is the way
With the forgiveness
That lay tortured and free...

•••

# THE END

Author & Poet Deborah Brooks Langford
When I was in 5th grade my teacher
introduced me to books.
Jane Eyre withering heights... etc...
I fell in love with books...
They took me on adventures and I would
daydream... And I started writing...
I have been writing poems all my life.
When I was in school I would write instead
of listen and dream of different poems and
stories. My passion is poetry
D2WP
Destiny to Write Publications
© SamothWolf Designs

www.ingramcontent.com/pod-product-compliance
Ingram Content Group UK Ltd.
Pitfield, Milton Keynes, MK11 3LW, UK
UKHW020210200726
13856UKWH00004B/1300